A Multitude of Stars

An anthology of micro poems

Lis McDermott

Copyright: © Lis McDermott 2021
Illustrator: © Lis McDermott 2021

Publisher: Pen & Ink Designs

ISBN: 9780993112911

Dedicated to all those who we have lost this year

A multitude of stars,
Glistening in the darkness;
Memories of lives lost.

Contents

WEATHER

WINTER

Winter, wet and damp
Clings to the trees and earth, whilst
Spring gently appears.

Grey, dull skies linger
Cold winds and rain rarely cease.
When will spring arrive?

The rains never stops
Flood barriers fail, as we
Watch settees sail by.

Hopelessly we watch
As black sludge invades our homes;
Mem'ries swept away.

The lack of sunlight
Urges me to hibernate.
Drowning, I feel SAD.

SPRING

Clouds
   Fluffy, soft
      Floating, gliding, moving
      Shapes in the blue.
      Candyfloss.

Forest
Abundant, verdant,
Willowy, twisted, arching,
Canopies beneath the skies.
Cathedrals.

Spring sun glimmers through dappled leaves, new life bursting forth into the world.

Feeling spring's warm sun;
Crisp air refreshes my soul
Singing of blue skies.

Early morning mist
Creeping coldness in dawn light
Ghosts of the past night.

SUMMER

Expanse of blue skies
Scorching shimmering heat haze
Summertime mirage.

Fields coloured purple
   Busy bees constantly buzz
    Towards lavender.

Summer breezes blow
Cooling my body heat as
I soak up the sun.

Abundant flowers
Bloom, rainbow colours, spreading
Floral aromas.

AUTUMN

On Halloween night
Monsters emerge from within
Ev'ryone of us.

Midnight; darkness falls
Shadows glide and shimmer with
Intended evil.

Innocent pumpkins
　　Gutted, carved, gouged, justified
　　　Halloween slaughter?

Morning mist whiteout
Shrouds the whole neighbourhood in
Deep, peaceful silence.

WINTER

Empty shadows fall
Darkly chilling our hearts, deep
With each frozen breath.

Lamplight shines orange,
Ornate patterns emerge from
white icy snowstorm.

New Year brings wonders,
A cornucopia of
Possibilities.

Crimson tides of the moon,
move silent in the dark skies.

Icy mist chills air
freezing frosty, fingers spread;
Decorating my whole world.

CHANGING WORLD

Nature's returning,
Less cars, less pollution, lets
Continue the change.

Retaliation.
Doomed by our lack of care, the
Earth's overheating.

Apocalyptic.
We live day-to-day; stars of
Our own doomsday films.

Daily risking their lives
Supporting our elderly
Caring from their hearts.

On days like today when the sun is
bright
The air sharp, only just warm;
My heart soars, and I feel elation;
I am alive.

Isolation
Solitude, calm
Learning, rejuvenating, resting
Time to slow down
Serenity.

Sitting in silence,
lost in my dreams of utopian
tomorrows

LOVE – LOST & FOUND

Were the tears in your eyes,
Mists of rain,
Or the residue of summers
melancholy
Seeping from your heart?

Tears fall;
   torrential showers from my heart.

Walking on beaches,
We search for heart-shaped pebbles,
Love carved memories.

You walked away,
  the shape of my hand
    remained on your heart;
      a dust of snow
        transformed by your coldness.

Each new day we wake,
offers you the chance to say 'sorry'.
Each day, hopeful, I wait.
Maybe tomorrow.

Fireworks

When our skins or lips touch,
Each neuron within my body
Explodes;
Fire bursts through my veins;
Electricity spirals in my brain;
My entire being floats and spins,
We are dazzled by our synapse.
In your presence I am forever
Glowing.

You are my passion.
My heart full, brimming with love
Eternal; souls wed.

You looked into my eyes,
Our souls recognised kin.
Without being lost
We were found
Without needing to ask
We both reached out.
Joys, minds, desires and passions
   collided.
We embraced each other's lives.
Living, breathing harmony.
Soul-mates in time.

Fireflies match the moon
Casting light on your features
Force your eyes to shine,
Sparkle above our bodies
Making love amidst their glow.

Loved by you, every breath taken,
I inhale stardust.

Amidst the bending boughs,
I linger, languishing in the
Labyrinth of leaf-filled tendrils.
Wool-gathering by the weeping
   willow;
Indulging in idealistic daydreams,
Deceitful and deluded,
Allowing myself to wallow in abject
   sadness
Lovelorn, lost in
Aimless abandonment.

Rain Talks

Gentle showers whisper
  Onto my window
    Trickling silently downwards
  Creating deep pools
Of heartfelt pain.

Licking water from
Your nipples, dripping slowly,
Onto my taste buds,
My lips, covet their goodness
like cool, raspberry ice-cream.

In beauty, you stand leaning against
the colonnade,
No longer naked, but dressed in red,
silken brocade,
Evidence of our rendezvous, your
bed, crumpled, unmade;
Lamenting the arrival of dawn, birds
sing an aubade,
My heart yearns for a repeat of our
lovemaking serenade.

Friendship
Constant like the sun, moon and
  stars,
The ebb and flowing tides of oceans,
Like foundations of a house
Dependable, faithfully supportive.
A bond held safe in my heart

Longing to hold you
My friends, in an embrace so
Warm, and loving for
As long as I need to feel
Unbound love to fill our veins.

Our love deepens, as understanding
grows;
Memories fill our goblets with
abundance
As we live life, moving forward
together.

You are my everything
Even a second of your absence
Turns day into the darkest night,
Birds singing in treetops cease
Sea tides slow, becalmed
And my breathing shallows.

You soothe me
However sad,
Whatever my fears,
The music of your voice
The calmness of your touch
Sings to my soul.

Your eyes fill
    With moonlight
        As we say our
            Last farewell.

GRIEF AND DEATH

My tears fall for you....
A life sacrificed too soon

My tears fall for your mother....
Outliving her only son,

My tears fall for your children
Born after your departing.

Dead Leaves
Translucent skin, veins, roads to
  nowhere,
Memories of my mother's wedding
  veil,
Delicate, lacy,
Returned to the earth.

I ask for no monument of stone
'In Memorium', but trees,
growing tall
A biodegradable tree pod,
Ashes and soil mixed;
Reaching skyward, entwined
With my lover's branches;
May my words drift, like leaves
Pages fluttering to the forest floor;
Poems recited by friends,
Recalling my laughter.

In death we live on
  Through those we meet in life with,
  Our words, actions, love.

Life is a mix of
Unexpected adventures
Set to challenge you;
You sink into an abyss
Or you take wings and fly high

BLACK & WHITE

Black are the hearts of
Oppressive governments who
Sanction racism.

Black History Month,
Chosen by someone who says
They don't see colour?
Lack of knowledge; shouldn't we
Learn Black history all year?

INNER LIVES

Stepping out beyond
I'm channelling my inner
Lioness; fearless.

Our core;
  Undulating
    Souls governed by the tides,
      Fluidity shapes our essence;
      Water.

Night
Nocturnal dreams,
Trolling your internal terrors,
When monsters invade your mind,
Invoked by psychedelic infused
Visions of nightmare worlds,
Memories of the past,
Fears of the future;
Creatures and events
Distorting into surreal truths.
Vanquished only
By the light of breaking dawn,
Returning sanity and reality.

Striped back, bare,
Exposed with every expression
Each exaggerated gesture,
Each vocal shrug,
Lascivious shaping of my lips,
Pronounced curls of my tongue,
I bared my soul, exhibiting
The sound of my naked voice.

When Shame consumes your
conscience
You feel humiliated to your core,
Each encounter causes anxiety
Peoples' stares mortify you;
Your whole life eclipsed.

Turquoise tells me tales at night
Sweeping flashes of turquoise,
Vivid brightness,
In streaks of lightness
Travel through my mind
Blinding the darkness of my dreams.
Interruptions,
Dazzling, luminosities midst
slumbers,
Meandering oceans of midnight
Invading my fantasies.

Pagliacci, Smokey Robinson
And so many more,
Jesters hide their emotions
Behind their smiles
Facades to conceal the sadness deep
    within;
Alone on stage, their damaged souls,
    momentarily
Appeased by the laughter and
    applause,
Burying their truths;
Behind their smiles
Lay the tears of a clown.

We writers shape our words,
Minds free
To roam our inner depths,
Our thoughts, hopes, fears
And dreams.
Our pens become our healer,
Our tool for mental freedom,
Aiding our words to bleed
From within our souls.

AND RELAX...

Babe, gently sleep
In the dusky arms of
Night's glowing moon.

Coffee kisses baked
In kitchens of a past life,
Small dollops of cake,
Lovingly, coffee-cream filled.
Nostalgia; recalling Mum.

I forgot that today was today,
and thought it was yesterday,
but then thought that it was the next
day,
which meant that it was in fact,
TODAY

New lunar diet;
On the moons silver highlands
You weigh a third less.

On your feet
  You can tap out a beat;
   You can run or walk
    Make your feet talk,
      You can prance and dance,
       And take a great leap
        But most of all
         You can keep
          That funky beat!

Turquoise colours of greens and blue,
Undulating waves, rise and swell
Resplendent in watery majesty
Quintessentially, heaven sent;
Underwater, turquoise star fish, cling to
Oceans reefs, beneath
Incandescent swathes of water, coloured
     deepest blue,
Sparkling, sunlit, creating tranquillity
     and
Endlessly, calming my soul.

LIMERICKS

The drummer boy played for a
marching band
To his drumming they marched
across the land.
But he could not keep the beat
So, they tripped over their feet,
The band didn't know when to move
or stand.

The leading man was played by a
horse,
And the role was a real tour de force.
But all he could say
Was a meagre 'neigh'
So, the audience all left, of course!

There was a carnivorous squirrel
Who went by the name of Red Cyril
His own secret tree
Kept him safe and free
From all of the lawmen in Wirral

I once met a boy from Yokohama
I have to say he was a real charmer,
He took me on a date,
But sadly, 'twas our fate
He gave all his love to his pet Llama

There once was a young girl called
Claire.
Whose skin was incredibly fair,
She got burned on her nose
And right down to her toes,
Joined the nudists and just didn't
care.

A Lothario called Goldie, a fish,
Always hankered after his dream, a
wish
To sunbathe by the pool,
With hot babes, looking cool.
Overheated, he was served in a dish.

ACKNOWLEDGEMENTS

With special thanks to:

Ryan Warner for inviting me to be part of his community on Instagram (@RDWworld), and opening my horizons as to the subjects I was writing about. He is an incredible advocate for poets.

I also have to say a special thanks to my wonderful online poetry group, the members of Lis' Poetry Place. I have loved working with you this year; reading your poetry; sharing all things poetic, and getting to know you all: -
Ann, Carolyne, Cat, Greeshma, Helen and Naman.

An extra-special thanks to my friend, Ann Brady for her support in getting this book published.

ABOUT THE AUTHOR

Lis McDermott was born in Leicestershire, but has lived in the South West of England since 1976. She now lives in Royal Wootton Bassett with her husband Conrad.

After formal training as a musician, Lis trained as a teacher and worked in Music Education for 34 years, latterly as a school's adviser. She also lectured in Music Education, and delivered some training both nationally and in Hong Kong. Lis co-authored a music scheme with a musical friend during the early 90's.

In 2008, she set up her own professional photography business, which closed in March 2020.

Having already written and published 5 books of her own, Lis decided to embrace her author persona, and began mentoring other writers. She is also presently working on her first novel.

As a lover of poetry Lis runs a monthly online poetry group.

www.LisMcDermottauthor.co.uk

Read more by Lis McDermott:

Changing Lives – Eight Short Stories
Mixed Feelings – An Autobiography
A Tilted View – An Anthology of poems
Blossom Falls – An Anthology of poems
Lis' Little Book of Limericks – An Anthology
                                    Of Poems

All available on Amazon